Penguin Readers

WOMEN WHO CHANGED THE WORLD

LEVEL

4

WRITTEN BY SUE LEATHER
SERIES EDITOR: SORREL PITTS

PENGUIN BOOKS

UK | USA | Canada | Ireland | Australia
India | New Zealand | South Africa

Penguin Books is part of the Penguin Random House group of companies
whose addresses can be found at global.penguinrandomhouse.com.
www.penguin.co.uk www.puffin.co.uk www.ladybird.co.uk

Penguin
Random House
UK

First published 2019
003

Text written by Sue Leather

Printed in China

A CIP catalogue record for this book is available from the British Library

ISBN: 978-0-241-37528-0

All correspondence to:
Penguin Books
Penguin Random House Children's
One Embassy Gardens, 8 Viaduct Gardens, London SW11 7BW

MIX
Paper from
responsible sources
FSC® C018179
FSC
www.fsc.org

Contents

New words

astronaut

athlete/athletics

judge

judo

magazines

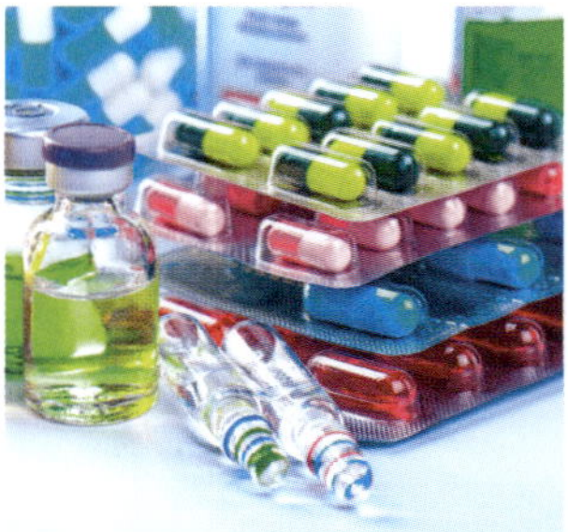

medicine

pilot

stadium

statue

university

vote

Note about the book

This book is about women around the world who have helped to change people's lives. The stories are about women who work in **education***, **politics**, **science** and sport. Some of the women have won the Nobel Prize, which is given to people who have achieved great things in politics, science or writing. Other women have worked with NASA – the part of the **government** of the United States of America that looks after the space **programme**. The stories are also about sportswomen who have won medals in the most important sporting event in the world, the Olympic Games.

You may already know some of these women, but many of them will be new to you. Women have achieved a lot in **history**, but sometimes the wonderful things that they have achieved have not been written about very much.

Before-reading questions

1 Look at the cover of this book. Do you know any of these women? What did they do?
2 Read the chapter titles on page 3. Which chapters look the most interesting to you? Why?
3 Choose two or three interesting women from history. Who were they, and what did they do?
4 What do you know about women's lives during World War Two?

*Definitions of words in **bold** can be found in the glossary on pages 77–79.

CHAPTER ONE

Women and education

"I do not wish for [women] to have power over men; but over themselves."
Mary Wollstonecraft (1759–1797)

Women's **rights** start with the **education** of girls and women. If we study the **history** of women's fight for **equality** with men, education has always been an important topic. It may be the most important topic, because women can only be **equal** to men if they have an equal education.

But the fight for equal education has met many problems. In many countries and at different times in history, girls had very little or no education. In the past, a lot of people believed that women were not as intelligent as men. People thought that a woman's only job was being a wife and mother. Why **educate** them for that? People worried that education was not good for women. In some places, people still have these ideas. The education of girls is still a very important topic around the world.

In the 18th and 19th **centuries**, people started to think, write and talk about women's education more and more.

Catherine the Great
(1729–1796)

There was **progress** in some countries. In 18th-century Russia, for example, Catherine the Great believed in education for everyone. In 1786, she started **free** education for all girls.

In England, writers like Catharine Macaulay, Mary Wollstonecraft, Hester Chapone and Hannah More all wrote about **female** education. At that time, girls from richer families only learned music, drawing, and maybe a little French and Italian. In her book *Letters on Education* (1790), Catharine Macaulay – the first English female **historian** – told mothers and fathers to educate their girls. Women could not do well, she said, because of their bad education.

Catharine Macaulay
(1731–1791)

One of the most important people of this time was Mary Wollstonecraft. She was an English thinker and writer who wrote about education and **social** equality for women. Her books have been very important for women's rights, and they are still important today.

Mary was born in London in 1759. Her family were

not rich, but they educated her. She taught at a school and also worked as a private teacher – she taught children in someone's house. She then wrote *Thoughts on the Education of Daughters* in 1787. In 1788, she began working for a London book **publisher**, who **published** her novel *Mary: A Fiction* (1788) and some of her other books. Her most famous book is *A Vindication of the Rights of Woman* (1792). In it, she writes that men and women must have equal education. Boys and girls, she wrote, must go to school together.

A Vindication of the Rights of Woman is very important in the history of women's rights. "Schools do not help girls and women," wrote Mary. With real education, she said, women could be good wives and mothers, but also good workers in many jobs.

Mary Wollstonecraft (1759–1797)

Her ideas were very new at the time. Other women wrote about better female education, but Mary's work was really important. She believed that education in Britain had to change. This kind of change could be good for all **society**.

Mary was writing about women and the vote a hundred years before women started fighting for it. Today, Mary Wollstonecraft is called "the mother of British feminism". Any woman who has the vote,

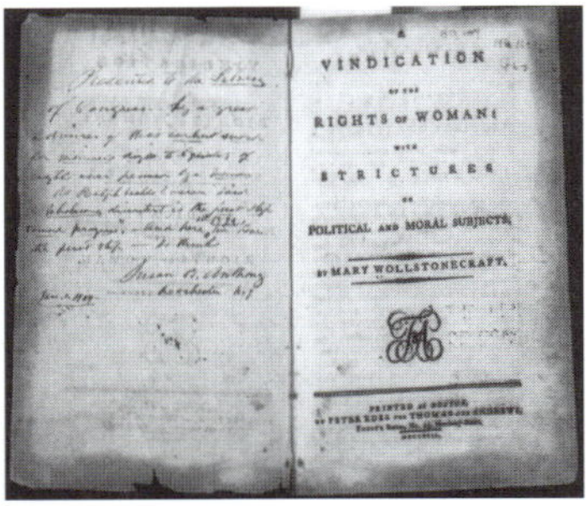

***A Vindication of the Rights of Woman* (1792)**

and can read and write, can say thank you to Mary Wollstonecraft.

In 2011, a group of people wanted to get money for a statue of Mary in London, so they put a picture of her on the Houses of Parliament. "We have a lot of statues of famous men. Let's have a statue of this famous woman!" they said.

In 2018, more people in **politics** and theatre joined the group to ask for a statue of Mary Wollstonecraft.

The fight that Mary Wollstonecraft started in the late 18th century is still not finished. Since then, many women have fought for female education – women like Margaret Bancroft and Jane Addams in the United States of America (USA), and Maria Montessori in Italy. In many places in the world, girls and women are still fighting for an equal education.

Mary Wollstonecraft's picture on the Houses of Parliament

Malala Yousafzai (1997–present)

One of the most famous fighters for girls' education today is Malala Yousafzai. Malala was born in 1997, in the Swat Valley in Pakistan. Her mother and father believed in education for girls. In 2007, a group of men called the Taliban came to the Swat Valley. They said, "People cannot have a television or play music." In January 2008, the Taliban said, "Girls cannot go to school."

Malala used the name "Gul Makai" and began writing for the BBC (the United Kingdom's television and radio) about life with the Taliban. She wrote about the last days before her school closed. Malala became famous, both in Pakistan and around the world, as a fighter for girls' education. She was brave, and she spoke about girls' education a lot. But the Taliban did not like it.

On 9th October 2012, a man from the Taliban got on to Malala's bus and shot Malala in the head and neck. Two of her friends were also hurt.

Malala did not die, but she was very badly hurt. She was taken to a hospital in the United Kingdom.

People in Pakistan and around the world hoped that she could get better. When Malala got better, she decided to continue her fight for girls' education.

In the next few years, Malala met with girls around the world, and she met with many **politicians**, like the **President** of the USA, Barack Obama. Everywhere she went, she talked about girls' education and equality.

In December 2014, Malala Yousafzai won the Nobel Peace Prize. She was only seventeen years old, and she was the youngest person ever to win it.

Today, Malala and her father, Ziauddin, work in many countries. They want to help to give girls an education. Malala has said, "I tell my story, not because it is **unique**, but because it is not. It is the story of many girls."

She is right. 130 million girls in the world do not go to school, and 15 million girls of primary-school age will never go into a classroom. This is because of things like war, or because girls have to get married when they are very young. In some countries, children have to work to get money for their family.

The education of girls is still an important problem for countries around the world. Educated women have better **health** and they work more, says the World Bank. They also do not have as many children, and they marry later. Countries where girls are educated are richer, too. Spending money on girls' education is very important if each country wants to become richer and happier.

As Malala has said, "One child, one teacher, one book, one pen can change the world."

Malala with President Obama and his family

CHAPTER TWO

Women and human rights

What are human rights? Having human rights means that we are all equal in society. We are born with our human rights. They are the same for every person.

Examples of human rights are the right to vote; the right to think and speak **freely**; and the right to free education. Human rights mean that people are not put into prison because they do not agree with the **government**, and that people are not hurt when they are in prison. It does not matter what **gender** or **race** you are, or how rich you are – you have the same rights. Human rights are a very important part of **democracy**.

There have been many women who have fought for human rights in different countries. In the USA, a lot of black women have fought for **freedom**. One of the early fighters was Harriet Tubman (1820–1913). Harriet was born a slave in Maryland – this means that she and her family were not free. When she was twelve years old, she was working in the fields. She could not read or write, but she was very intelligent.

From a young age, Harriet knew that she wanted to be free. She also knew that she had to help other slaves to find freedom.

Harriet Tubman
(1820–1913)

At this time, there were slaves in the south of the USA, but not in the north. In 1849, Harriet ran away to find freedom in the north. But she did not stay there. She went back to the south and helped to free other slaves. First she helped her family, and then she helped others. She was very brave. She often spoke about the freedom of the slaves and women's rights. She started schools for free slaves because she knew that education was important. Later, she also fought for the vote for women.

Harriet Tubman **led** the way for another famous fighter for human rights, Rosa Parks. Rosa Parks was born in Alabama in 1913. She is famous because she did not stand up! When Rosa was a young woman, in many places in the USA, black people – who were called "coloureds" at that time – and white people could not sit together.

Rosa Parks (1913–2005)

From a young age, Rosa knew that "there was a black world and a white world," as she said later. One of the places where black people and white people did not mix was on buses. Rosa Parks worked at a shop in the city of Montgomery, Alabama. On 1st December 1955, after a long day's work at the shop, Rosa Parks got on the bus to go home. She sat in a seat for "coloured" people. In those days, there was a line on the floor of the bus. White people sat in the front of the line, and black people had to sit behind it. This meant that, when a black person caught the bus, they had to get on at the front of the bus to pay. Then they had to get off and get on the bus again at the back door.

On this day in December, the bus began to fill with white people. After a short time, the bus was full, and the driver noticed that some white people were standing up. The driver stopped the bus and asked four black people to stand up. This meant that the white people could sit down.

Three of the black people on Rosa's bus stood up, but Rosa did not. She continued sitting. The driver asked, "Why don't you stand up?" Rosa replied, "I don't think I should have to stand up." The driver called the police, and Rosa was **arrested**. What Rosa did on that bus was very important in the fight for black people's rights in the USA.

Today, there are still many women fighting for human rights in different parts of the world. In Iran, there is Shirin Ebadi. Shirin was born in the city of Hamadan,

Shirin Ebadi (1947–present)

Iran, in 1947. In 1969, she got a degree in **law** from the University of Tehran. She later got a PhD – a higher degree – in law, and she became Iran's first woman judge. In 1975, she became the first president of the Tehran city **court**.

Later, Iran's government stopped women from becoming judges. Shirin lost her job as the president of the city court, and she had to work as a secretary.

For years, Shirin Ebadi fought to work in law. In 1993, she was able to be a **lawyer** again.

She helped many people in prison, and she stopped them from getting hurt by the prison workers. In 2003, Shirin was given the Nobel Peace Prize for her work in democracy and human rights, and for fighting for the rights of women and children. The Nobel Committee said she was a brave person who never worried that she was in danger. Now, she travels around the world speaking about human rights.

Rigoberta Menchú is also an important woman who fought for the rights of **Indigenous** people in her country. Rigoberta was born in 1959 to a poor K'iche' Maya (Indigenous) family in a small village in Guatemala.

When she was young, she helped with the family's farm work. Sometimes, she worked in the mountains

Rigoberta Menchú (1959–present)

where her family lived. Sometimes, she went with other children and adults to pick coffee on big farms near the Pacific sea. But she went to school, too.

After leaving school, Rigoberta worked against human rights crimes by Guatemalan soldiers from 1960 to 1996, during a war in the country. In 1979 and 1980, her brother Petrocinio and her mother, Juana, were killed by Guatemalan soldiers. Her father, Vicente, died in the 1980 burning of the Spanish Embassy. In 1984, her brother Victor was also killed by soldiers.

In 1981, Rigoberta ran away from Guatemala because living there was dangerous for her. She went to live in Mexico. In 1995, she married Ángel Canil, a Guatemalan. They have a son, Mash Nahual J'a. While in Mexico, Rigoberta continued to fight for Indigenous people's rights in Guatemala. In 1992, she got the Nobel Peace Prize for her work.

Rigoberta and these other women have fought for the rights of women, but also for the rights of all humans.

CHAPTER THREE

Women and the vote

"If we win . . . this hardest of all fights, then . . . in the future it is going to be made easier for women all over the world to win their fight when their time comes." Emmeline Pankhurst (1858–1928)

The fight for the vote was one of the greatest fights that women have had. It started in the 19th century and continued into the 20th century. In the 1890s, parts of New Zealand and Australia were the first places to give women the vote. The first country in Europe to allow women to vote was Finland, which was then part of Russia. Finland also had the world's first women **Members of Parliament** (**MPs**), in 1907. After Finland came Norway, which gave the vote to women in 1913. Denmark followed in 1915.

In the United Kingdom, the vote did not come until 1918. The fight for votes there was led by some very brave women. The most famous is a woman called Emmeline Pankhurst. She was the **leader** of the "suffragettes" – the name of a group of women who fought for the vote.

Emmeline was born in 1858 in Manchester in the north of England. Her father had a small business, and they lived in a large house. Both her mother and her father believed in women's rights.

Emmeline was the oldest of ten children. She was

Emmeline Pankhurst
(1858–1928)

very intelligent and could read when she was three years old. In Emmeline's time, girls were not given a very good education. They learned things they needed for family life, like how to cook. But Emmeline's mother and father had money. When she was older, they paid for her to go to a women's school in Paris. When she came back five years later, at twenty years old, she could speak good French and knew how to cook, but she also knew **chemistry**.

In 1879, Emmeline married a lawyer called Richard Pankhurst. Richard also believed in the vote for women. He wrote some laws in 1870 and 1882 that allowed women to keep their money or houses after they married. Emmeline and Richard had five children between 1880 and 1889. Emmeline and Richard believed in the same ideas. When he died in 1898, Emmeline was very sad.

In 1889, Emmeline started the Women's Franchise League, which fought for married women to vote in **elections**. In 1903, she helped to start the Women's Social and Political Union (WSPU), which became famous. They believed in doing things, not only saying words. The WSPU were the first "suffragettes".

Emmeline's daughters, Christabel and Sylvia, were also

suffragettes. In Britain, politicians, the newspapers and the people were very surprised by what the suffragettes did. The women walked in the streets and broke windows. They burned buildings. When they were put in prison, they did not eat. In 1913, a suffragette called Emily Davison was killed when she threw herself under the king's horse at a famous horse race. She did this because the government would not give women the right to vote. The suffragettes said, "Emily died for women."

Emmeline was a very good speaker. She went to the USA and gave many talks there. The most famous one was called "Freedom or Death". It was about how strong the suffragettes were.

Emmeline talked about "we women of England". She said, "The men who are against us have to choose between giving us freedom, or giving us death."

Emmeline Pankhurst speaking in New York, 1911

Some people did not like what the suffragettes were doing. But Emmeline and the other women knew that they had to do something. They couldn't just talk about things. Emmeline, like many of the suffragettes, was put in prison many times. From 1908 to 1909, she was in

Suffragette poster showing a woman being forced to eat, 1905

prison three times. From 1912 to 1913, she was in prison twelve times. She was very brave, and she knew that women had to win this fight. She even stopped eating. Sometimes, the police **forced** her to eat, which was very painful. Sometimes, the suffragettes almost died from not eating, but still they continued to fight. At times, the suffragettes also chained themselves outside 10 Downing Street – where the British **prime minister** lives – shouting "Votes for women!"

There were also some men who fought for a woman's right to vote. Two examples were Members of Parliament Keir Hardie and George Lansbury, who both agreed with the suffragettes. Winston Churchill – who later became prime minister – started his **career** against the vote for women, but later he agreed with it. Maybe this was because his wife, Clementine, agreed with it.

In 1918, women over thirty got the vote after many years of fighting. Emmeline died on 14th June 1928, at the age of sixty-nine. On 2nd July 1928, women were given equal voting rights with men – they could vote at the age of twenty-one. Emmeline did not live to see it.

In 1999, *Time* magazine called Emmeline Pankhurst one of the 100 most important people of the 20th century. They wrote that she changed society very much.

What about today? In the 20th century, women in many countries fought for the vote and got it. Little by little, women have got the vote in almost every country in the world.

Years that the vote was given to all women

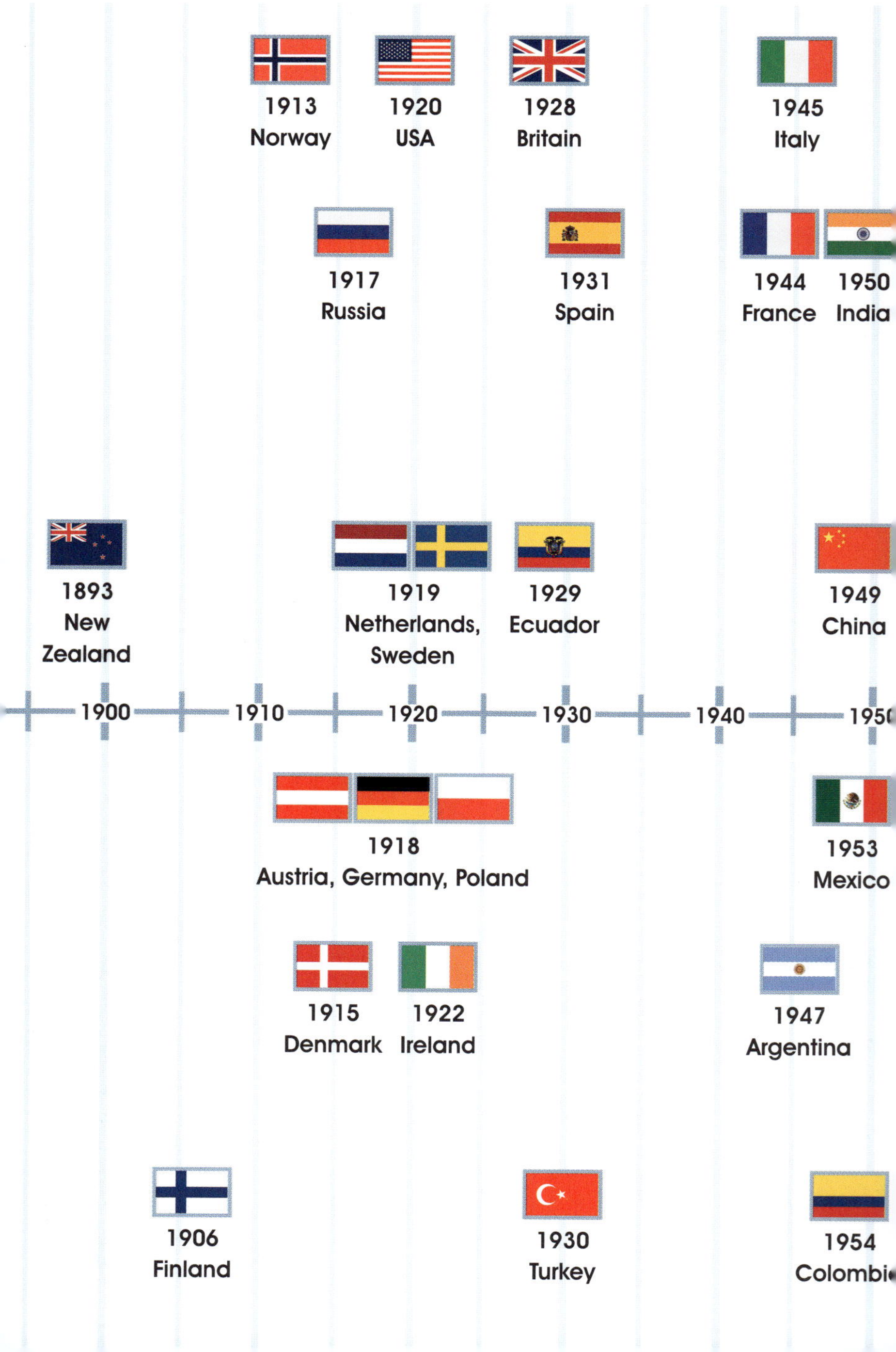

in a selection of countries*

1963
Iran, Morocco

1990
Samoa

2011
Saudi Arabia

1960
Canada
Some women were given the vote in 1918, but Asian and Indigenous women were excluded from voting at that time*.

1994
South Africa
From 1930, only white women were allowed to vote*.

1957
Malaysia, Zimbabwe

1974
Jordan

1993
Moldova

2005
Kuwait

1960 – 1970 – 1980 – 1990 – 2000 – 2010

1962
Algeria

1971
Switzerland

1989
Namibia

2006
United Arab Emirates

1962
Australia
Some women were given the vote in 1902, but Indigenous women were excluded from voting until 1962*.

1964
Libya

1976
Portugal

1994
Kazakhstan

* Many countries gave the vote to some women earlier than the years shown here, but these dates show the years all women were given equal voting rights to men.

Saudi Arabia is the newest country to give women the vote, in 2011. In 2015, women there voted for the first time in town and city elections.

Hatoon al-Fassi was one of the first Saudi Arabian women to vote. The Saudi **professor** and women's rights leader was driven to the voting station because women were not allowed to drive in 2015. She voted in an almost-empty building, which was for women only.

"It feels great," she said as she came out, with a very big smile. "This is a very important moment. I thank God that I am living it." She fought for that day for more than ten years.

Saudi Arabian women voting for the first time

Hatoon al-Fassi (1964–present)

This was progress for Hatoon al-Fassi and for Saudi Arabian women, but still only 10% of Saudi's voters in the 2015 elections were women. In Saudi Arabia and some other countries, like Pakistan, it is difficult for women to go out to vote. But, from June 2018, women in Saudi Arabia were allowed to drive themselves. This may mean that higher numbers of women will vote in the future.

Women have made a lot of progress in the last 100 years. In most countries, they can now vote. This is thanks to brave women like Emmeline Pankhurst and Hatoon al-Fassi who fought so hard and won.

CHAPTER FOUR

Women and feminism

When we use the word "feminism", we are talking about a number of political and social **movements** and ideas that have one **goal**. That goal is to achieve equality between all people. All over the world, **feminist** movements have fought, and are still fighting, for women's right to vote. These movements are also fighting for women's right to work, to **earn** equal pay and to own property. They are fighting for women to get an education and for women to have equal rights when they get married. **Feminists** have also worked hard to stop **sexual assault** and other crimes against women at work and at home.

Feminism is not new. It has a long history in the West and in other parts of the world.

The history of modern feminism comes in four "**waves**" – or movements. Each wave looked at different parts of the same problem. The first wave, in the late 19th and early 20th centuries, was mostly about women's right to vote. The second wave, which began in the 1960s, was about women's fight for freedom. During this time, women fought for equality in the law and in society. The third wave, which began in the 1990s, continues the work of second-wave feminism. In it, women want to be "themselves". They fight to be different from how some men want to see them, and from other women.

The fourth wave started around 2012, and it is about sexual **harassment** and crimes against women at work. It uses a lot of social media – like Facebook, YouTube and Twitter – and has been led by the **#MeToo** movement.

The first wave of feminism in the West was mostly about getting the vote. Women in northern Europe and in places like the United Kingdom, the USA and Australia were all fighting for the vote in the last years of the 1890s and the early years of the 20th century.

But, during these times, countries like China, Egypt and Iran had feminist movements, too. For example, the Iranian Women's Movement wanted to achieve women's equality in education, **marriage**, careers and law. In Egypt, in 1923, Huda Shaarawi started the Egyptian Feminist Union. She was the leader of the Arab women's rights movement.

Huda Shaarawi (1879–1947)

The second wave of feminism arrived in the middle of the 20th century. Second-wave feminism was about more than the vote; it was about **sexuality**, family and work. Second-wave feminism also talked about sexual assault against women. It brought changes in laws about **divorce** and children.

All over the world, feminists fought to change family laws that gave husbands control over their wives. In many European countries, married women still had very few rights. For example, in France, married women could not work if their husbands did not agree to it. That law only changed in 1965.

One of the greatest European women at this time was a French **philosopher**, thinker and writer called Simone de Beauvoir.

Simone de Beauvoir was born in Paris in 1908. She studied **philosophy** at the Sorbonne, the famous university in Paris. De Beauvoir was only the ninth woman to study at the Sorbonne at the time. In 1929, when she was twenty-one years old, she met Jean-Paul Sartre, the philosopher. They were together for fifty-one years, until he died in 1980. They never lived together, never married and never had children. She spent her life writing and thinking.

Simone de Beauvoir (1908–1986)

Simone de Beauvoir wrote her most famous work, *Le Deuxième Sexe* (*The Second Sex*), in 1949. In it, she said, "One is not born, but rather becomes, a woman." With this famous sentence, Simone was the first thinker to write about sex and gender. We are born as a sex – either as a boy or girl, she said. But our gender is made by our society. As we grow, society teaches us how to act like women. Women, said Simone, are always described as "The Other" – she means that women do not act like men, and, because of this, men believe that women are not as important as them.

Simone wrote a large number of books. Her thoughts about women in society are still very important today.

Later in the 20th century, writers like Betty Friedan and Gloria Steinem from the USA and Germaine Greer from Australia continued Simone's work. In 1963, Betty Friedan's book *The Feminine Mystique* was published. It showed that some American women were not happy if they only worked at home. They were not happy just cooking and looking after the children. People really liked the book, and Betty talked about it all over the world. Ten years after her book was published, more than half of the workers in the West were women. The world was changing fast.

Betty Friedan (1921–2006)

Countries in the West are not the only countries that have important feminist writers and thinkers. In the Arab world, Nawal El Saadawi is very famous. Nawal is a doctor and writer from Egypt. She has written many books about women in **Islam**. In the 1980s, she spent a lot of time in prison because of her work. In her book, *Memoirs from a Women's Prison* (1983), she wrote, "Danger has been a part of my life ever since I picked up a pen and wrote. Nothing is more **perilous** than truth in a world that lies." People have called her "the Simone de Beauvoir of the Arab World".

Nawal El Saadawi (1931–present)

The third and fourth waves of feminism, from the 1990s until today, have often been about women's fight against sexual harassment and assault, and the fight to be "themselves". Women's sexuality is important in these feminist waves. These waves are also about the sexism that happens to women every day. Fourth-wave feminism uses social media to talk about the problem of harassment in the street and at work. It also talks about sexual assault in universities and colleges.

Examples of fourth-wave feminism are: the 2017 Women's March; the 2018 Women's March; and the #MeToo movement. The #MeToo movement talks about famous men who have hurt or **harassed** women. Many men in the film and TV business have been **accused** of harassing women, and of sexual assault.

Today, English woman Laura Bates is an important feminist. After studying English Literature at the University of Cambridge, Laura looked after other people's children. She learned that the young girls she looked after were already worried about how their bodies looked. She set up the Everyday Sexism Project website in 2012 after finding it difficult to speak out about sexism. The project shows that sexism happens to women every day in many ways. Women from all over the world can write to the website about the things that happen to them.

Laura Bates (1986–present)

Today, some people say that women have won the fight for equality. But it's not true; women all over the world are still fighting for their rights.

CHAPTER FIVE

Women and work

In the past, almost all women worked at home. They did cooking and cleaning, and they looked after children. In some places in the world, that still happens.

When women started to do paid work in the 19th and early 20th centuries, almost half of it was cleaning and cooking in other people's homes. It was hard, dirty work, and there was not much free time. Women often lived in very small rooms. New jobs that appeared in factories, shops and offices were better. But women earned half the money that was paid to men for the same jobs. They also worked long hours and got very low pay – and it was very hard work.

Women working at a house in Northamptonshire, England

Women making guns, London, 1917

During this time, women also became teachers or nurses. But people thought that this work was not important, and women had to leave their jobs when they married.

War is usually a bad thing, but it has sometimes been good for women and work. In World War One (1914–1918), men left home to fight, and women were needed to work both in the army and in their home country.

World War Two (1939–1945) gave millions of jobs to women in the USA and in the United Kingdom. Thousands of American and British women joined the army. Although almost none of them carried a gun, they did "men's" jobs and got the same pay. At the same time, millions of men left their jobs to fight the war in Europe and other places. This meant that women had to go out to work because they needed to feed their children.

"Rosie the Riveter" poster, used by the US government to get women to go to work

After the war ended and the men came home, more than 2 million women lost their jobs. In the USA and the United Kingdom, women had to return home. Newspapers and magazines told women to keep a nice, clean home while their husbands were at work. They showed the home as a woman's place. There were still jobs for women, but they were usually in shops or for secretaries. However, the number of women working outside the home was still higher than before. This was because a lot of men did not come home from the war, so women had to work to look after their families.

In the 1950s, many countries in the West became quite rich. Factories were making lots of new things, and this meant there were new jobs for women. In the 1950s and 1960s, the number of women who worked outside the home went up again.

Niloofar Rahmani (1992–present), Afghanistan's first female pilot

In the 1970s, women began to go to colleges and universities to study. More women were going to college and wanted to go out to work. This was a change from women in the past, who only worked a little because they got married and had children. In the West, doctors could help women to choose how many children they had. Families became smaller.

Today, the number of women at work continues to go up. In 2014 in Canada, for example, over 47% of workers were women. Today, in many countries, women need to go out to work to help their families. They are also going into "men's" jobs – these days there are women pilots, judges and astronauts!

Women are now working in large numbers, and they are also becoming leaders in business and politics.

One of these leaders is Sheryl Sandberg, who is the Chief Operating Officer (COO) of Facebook.

Sheryl Sandberg (1969–present)

Sheryl was born in Washington D.C., and she got an MBA from Harvard Business School. She worked for Google before becoming the first woman COO at Facebook.

In 2012, she was named in the *Time* 100, a list of the 100 most important people in the world. In 2013, Sheryl wrote her first book, *Lean In: Women, Work, and the Will to Lead*. *Lean In* is a book to help women to achieve their career goals. It is also for men who want to make a more equal society.

Women are becoming leaders in business, but equal pay is still a big problem. In the USA in 2016, women earned about 82 cents for every dollar a man made. In the United Kingdom, more than three out of four businesses pay men more than women. In many jobs, men earn 10% more than women earn.

In 2018, it was discovered that the BBC was paying some men a lot more than women for the same jobs. One of the women who spoke about the problem was Carrie Gracie.

Carrie Gracie worked in China for the BBC. She speaks the language and knows a lot about China. She has worked for the BBC for thirty years. In January 2018, she left her job in China because the BBC were paying women less than men. After a long fight, the BBC paid Carrie the same amount of money as the men were paid.

Carrie Gracie (1962–present)

The fight for work and equal pay has not been won. Women still do most of the work in the home, which means that many of them are working a lot more than men. In many parts of the world, women cannot work outside of the house, or cannot work where they want to. They are often paid less, and sexism and sexual harassment at work are a problem every day. Women are 50% of the world's people, and, when they cannot work, it is a big problem for the world.

CHAPTER SIX

Women and science

There have been women in **science** for many hundreds of years. Some women were working in medicine, for example, in early times. Even in Ancient Greece, women were able to study science.

In these early times, the number of women in science was not high. But, in the 20th century, women started to study and work in science more and more. One of the big names of the 20th century was a woman from Poland named Marie Curie. She was one of the most famous scientists the world has ever known.

Marie Curie (1867–1934)

In 1903, Marie Curie was given the Nobel Prize in **Physics** with her husband, Pierre, for their work on **radioactivity**. In 1911, she won the Nobel Prize in Chemistry without her husband.

She was the first woman to win a Nobel Prize, and she is the only woman to win the Nobel Prize for two different topics.

Who was this great woman?

Marie Skłodowska was born in 1867 in Warsaw, Poland. Her parents were teachers who believed in the education of women. When she was a young woman, she moved to Paris to study. There she met Pierre Curie, who became her husband. They were both working with radioactivity. Pierre died in an accident in 1906, but Marie continued their work.

In Marie Curie's time, science was a man's world. She was the first woman to achieve big things in this world. She was also the first woman to get a PhD from a French university, and she was the first woman to become a professor at the University of Paris.

Marie Curie with Albert Einstein and other men scientists

Today, we know that Marie Curie was a Nobel Prize-winning scientist. But we must remember that it almost did not happen! In 1903, the French Academy of Sciences wrote a letter to the Nobel Committee. They wanted Pierre Curie and another man to win the Nobel Prize in Physics.

Marie Curie's name was not there! Then, a Swedish professor of mathematics called Gösta Mittag-Leffler, who was on the Nobel Committee, wrote a letter to Pierre Curie. "Marie Curie worked on the research too, didn't she?" he asked. So Pierre wrote back to the Nobel Committee. He and Marie had to be thought about together "for our research on radioactive bodies", he wrote. That is why the Nobel Prize was given to both Pierre and Marie.

Marie Curie's work was very important. She had important ideas about radioactivity and discovered polonium (Po) and radium (Ra). Polonium was named after her country, Poland. She opened the Curie Institutes in Paris and in Warsaw. They are still important places to study medicine today.

The Curies' work helped to make X-rays, which are very important in medicine today. During World War One, Marie helped to put X-ray machines in ambulances, which Marie herself drove to the places where they were needed. She worked for the International Red Cross and taught doctors how to use X-rays.

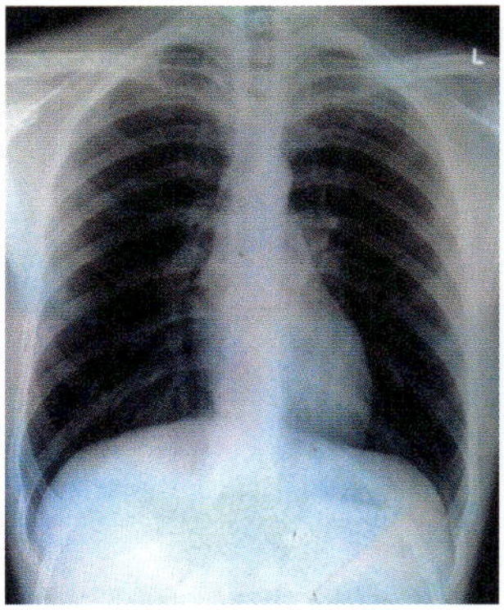

An X-ray

Marie was very good at this important and dangerous work.

But men scientists in France gave Marie a lot of problems, and she never got enough money for her work. At the end of the 1920s, Marie became very ill because of her work, and she died in 1934.

Later in the 20th century, there were more women in science, and some of them did very important work. However, they did not win any Nobel Prizes. For example, Lise Meitner (1878–1968) was an Austrian–Swedish scientist who worked on radioactivity and physics. Lise and Otto Hahn led the small group of scientists who first split the atom. Their work was published in 1939.

Lise Meitner (1878–1968)

Lise was very famous late in her life, but she was not given the 1944 Nobel Prize in Chemistry. That was given to Otto Hahn. Since then, many scientists and journalists have asked why Lise did not get the Nobel Prize. Was it because she was a woman?

Another woman who did not get a Nobel Prize is Rosalind Franklin. She was a British scientist who was born in 1920. Rosalind Franklin was very intelligent, and she knew when she was fifteen that she wanted to be a scientist. Her father did not want her to be a scientist because it was difficult for women, and he told her to study something different. But Rosalind did not listen, and she went to study science at the University of Cambridge.

Rosalind Franklin (1920–1958)

Rosalind is most famous for her work on DNA while at King's College, London. Her work helped other scientists discover how DNA is made. James Watson, Francis Crick and Maurice Wilkins got the Nobel Prize for this work in 1962.

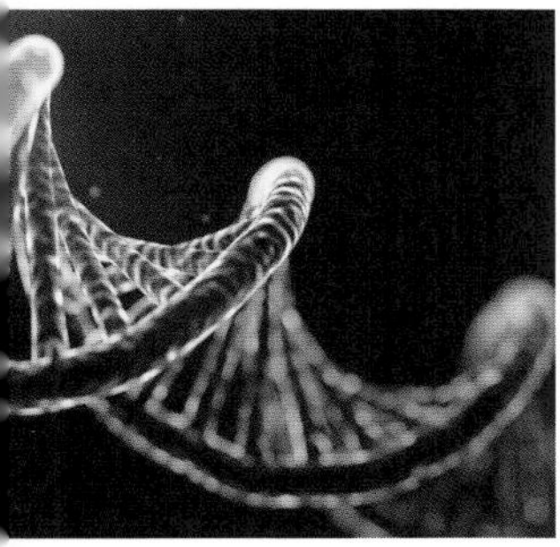

DNA

Rosalind died in 1958. Because the Nobel Prize can only be shared between three living scientists, Rosalind's work was not spoken about when the prize was given to James, Francis and Maurice. Many people believe that Rosalind, like Lise Meitner, did not get the Nobel Prize because she was a woman.

Since those days, a lot of female scientists have won the Nobel Prize – women like Barbara McClintock, Rita Levi-Montalcini and Gertrude B. Elion.

Tu Youyou
(1930–present)

Now, more and more women are entering science. Tu Youyou is a Chinese **chemist** who won the Nobel Prize in 2015. She is most famous for discovering a medicine for **malaria**, which has saved millions of lives.

Today, still only 30% of the world's scientists are women. But the numbers are getting higher. Now, there is a group of young women scientists who are doing wonderful things. American Emily Levesque is one of them. Emily is an astronomer – a scientist who studies the stars in the sky. Her work helps us to understand our world. She also teaches at the University of Washington, and she gives talks about her work. She loves answering questions from people who are not astronomers.

Emily Levesque
(1984–present)

More and more women are now going into science because of female scientists like Marie Curie, Rosalind Franklin and Emily Levesque.

CHAPTER SEVEN

Women and politics

We know that, in many countries, women started to get the vote in the first years of the 20th century. Their next step was to enter politics and become politicians. In the 20th century, women made some progress in this fight.

The Houses of Parliament, United Kingdom

Nancy Astor (1879–1964)

In the United Kingdom, the first woman to become a Member of Parliament was Nancy Astor, in 1919. Astor was born in Virginia, USA, in 1879. There were eight children in her family, and, when Nancy was young, they were very poor. Later, Nancy's father made a lot of money in business, and the children were able to get an education. As a child, Nancy loved reading, and she was very intelligent.

In the 1890s, Nancy met Robert Gould Shaw. They married in New York City in 1897 and had a son, Robert, a year later. But Nancy and her husband were not happy, and they **divorced** in 1903. Two years later, Nancy moved to England with her son and her sister Phyllis. In England, she became famous as an intelligent and beautiful American woman. In 1906, she married Waldorf Astor, who was also a politician.

Nancy became the first woman to sit in the House of Commons on 1st December 1919. In Parliament, she talked about women's rights. She was also very interested in children's health and education. When Nancy became an MP, women could only vote at the age of thirty. Nancy wanted women of twenty-one years old to vote. In 1928, women got the vote at twenty-one.

Nancy was very strong, and she always said what she thought. She did many things that women were not able to do before, like being an MP. She wanted to help other people. She said to the BBC, "I wanted the world to get better, and I knew it could not get better if it was going to be **ruled** by men." Nancy was an MP until 1945.

In Europe and North America, changes were happening fast. But the first woman prime minister didn't come from Europe or the USA. She came from Ceylon, a country that is now called Sri Lanka. On 21st July 1960, Sirimavo Bandaranaike became the first woman prime minister in the world.

Sirimavo came from a rich family, but she always wanted to help the poor people in her country.

She went into politics when her husband, Prime Minister Solomon Bandaranaike, was killed in 1959. She became the leader of the Sri Lanka Freedom Party (SLFP). One of Solomon Bandaranaike's cousins asked, "What does she know about politics?" "She only knows about the kitchen," said her friends. They thought it was a big mistake.

But they were wrong. Thanks to Sirimavo Bandaranaike, the name of Bandaranaike became very famous. She became the world's first woman prime minister, and she led her country's government three times. She changed Ceylon a lot, and she gave it the new name of Sri Lanka.

Sirimavo Bandaranaike (1916–2000)

The 20th century and the first part of the 21st century have seen big steps for women in politics. There have been many women leaders – women like Indira Gandhi in India, Golda Meir in Israel, and Margaret Thatcher and Theresa May in the United Kingdom. There has also been Ellen Johnson Sirleaf in Liberia, Julia Gillard in Australia, Tarja Halonen in Finland and Angela Merkel in Germany. These are a few of the women who have led or are leading their countries as prime ministers or presidents. In 2018, a woman was president or prime minister in sixteen countries.

In 2016, the USA almost had its first woman president with Hillary Clinton. Hillary was the First Lady of the United States from 1993 to 2001 because her husband, Bill Clinton, was president. Then she was US Senator for New York from 2001 to 2009, and US Secretary of State from 2009 to 2013, when Barack Obama was president. In 2016, the Democratic Party chose her to take part in the election of president of the USA. She won the "popular vote", which means that more of the Americans who voted, voted for her, but she was not **elected**.

Hillary Clinton (1947–present)

Hillary is a lawyer, and in her career she has worked hard for the rights of women and of families. In a talk in 1995, she said,

"Human rights are women's rights, and women's rights are human rights." She said that a country cannot be great if its women are not free. She spoke about the rights of women in the world. In countries where women do well, she said, everyone does well.

Hillary Clinton is an example of a woman who has achieved a lot in politics, and there are others. But, in many countries, it is still hard for women to enter into politics. Often, women have to choose between having a family and having a career. Also, politics has always been a career for men, and when women become politicians, some people say bad things to them.

Women still have a lot to do in politics. In 2018, for example, there were 650 MPs in the United Kingdom Parliament. Only 208 of them were women – that is 32%. And that is the highest number of women MPs in British history. This was 100 years after some women first got the vote and almost a hundred years after Nancy Astor entered Parliament.

Usually, in the world, the number of women in a country's parliament is 23%. But the numbers change a lot in different countries. For example, there are not many women in the Parliament of Sri Lanka. In 2017, four of the countries with the highest number of women in their parliaments were in Central and South America. They were Bolivia, Cuba, Nicaragua and Mexico. In 2017, Rwanda had more female MPs than any other country.

Jacinda Ardern (1980–present)

There are more and more women prime ministers and presidents in the world, and they are also becoming younger. In 2017, Jacinda Ardern became the prime minister of New Zealand when she was thirty-seven years old. She is the world's youngest female prime minister, and the fourth-youngest woman or man prime minister. She had a baby in 2018 and was only the second prime minister to have a baby while she was in the job. The other woman was Benazir Bhutto, prime minister of Pakistan, who had her baby in 1990. Jacinda Ardern has said, "I hope that one day this will not be interesting any more." She wants it to be normal for women to be in politics and to be mothers.

Half of the people who live in the world are women. Many people hope that, in the future, 50% of the world's governments will be women.

CHAPTER EIGHT

Women and flight

In 1903, Orville and Wilbur Wright flew the first aeroplane. Just five years later, in 1908, women pilots started flying. One of the first women to fly was a young woman called Amelia Earhart. She flew aeroplanes, and she was a writer. Earhart was the first woman to fly alone across the Atlantic Ocean.

Amelia Earhart was born in Kansas, USA. She saw her first aeroplane at the age of ten. She did not like it. "It looked not at all interesting," she said. Ten years later, she went with a friend to watch some pilots flying aeroplanes. A pilot saw them, and he flew his aeroplane down at them. Amelia was afraid, but she did not move. As the plane went by, she felt very excited. "I did not understand it at the time," she said later, "but I believe that little red aeroplane said something to me as it went by." In 1920, a pilot took her up in an aeroplane, and that changed her life. She said later, "When I was two or three hundred feet off the ground, I knew I had to fly."

Amelia Earhart
(1897–1937, disappeared)

In 1921, Amelia had lots of different jobs. She was a photographer and a lorry driver. She saved $1,000 for flying lessons. Later that year, she bought her first aeroplane. It was called "The Canary". The next year, she flew to 14,000 feet, higher than any other woman before. Amelia achieved a lot in the next few years. In 1932, she was the first woman to fly alone across the Atlantic, which she did in 14 hours and 56 minutes. She wrote a book, *The Fun of It*, about her journey. She loved to fly alone. In 1935, she was the first person to fly alone the 2,408 miles across the Pacific between Honolulu, Hawaii, and Oakland, California. She was the first person to fly alone from Los Angeles to Mexico City, which she did in 13 hours and 23 minutes. And she was the first person to fly alone without stopping from Mexico City to Newark, USA, which she did in 14 hours and 19 minutes.

These were just some of the things Amelia achieved. In 1937, as Amelia was close to her 40th birthday, she was ready for a big journey. She wanted to be the first woman to fly around the world.

On 1st June, Amelia and Fred Noonan left Miami and began their 29,000-mile journey around the world. When they came down in Lae, New Guinea, on 29th June, there were only 7,000 more miles to travel. Their next stop was Howland Island. Howland Island is 2,556 miles from Lae in the Pacific Ocean, and it is a very small island.

On 2nd July, at 10 a.m., Amelia and Fred started for Howland Island. They flew into grey skies and rain. In the early morning, Amelia called the *Itasca*, a US ship. She said there was cloudy weather. At 7:42 a.m., the *Itasca* got the message, "We are flying at 1,000 feet." The ship tried to reply, but Amelia's aeroplane did not hear it. At 8:45 a.m., Amelia spoke on the radio for the last time. Nobody heard from Amelia Earhart again. She and Fred disappeared. Nobody knows what happened to them.

People will remember Amelia Earhart because she was brave and because she achieved so much for women and **flight**. In a letter to her husband, George Putnam, during her last flight, she showed how brave she was. "Please know that I know about the dangers," she wrote. "I want to do it because I want to do it. Women must try to do things as men have tried."

After Amelia Earhart, there were many women pilots in the USA. Mary Wallace "Wally" Funk was one of them. She flew aeroplanes for her job at the age of twenty. But, in 1960, a space **programme** was started by an American man called William Randolph Lovelace, who worked at NASA. He had helped to choose the first seven astronauts. Those astronauts were all white men.

William thought that women should also be able to go into space. He knew that the Soviet Union wanted to have women astronauts, too. The USA wanted to be the first country to put women in space, so, in 1960, William began to **test** women in the USA as astronauts.

It was called the "Women in Space" programme. Thirteen women pilots were asked to join it, and Wally Funk was one of them.

Wally Funk (1939–present)

Wally Funk always wanted to be an astronaut. She, like the other women, had to do lots of difficult **tests**. In one test, the women were placed in special rooms with water where they could not hear anything or see anything. Funk was in there for 10 hours and 35 minutes. She tested better than John Glenn, the man who went to the Moon! She passed her tests and was ready to go into space. But the programme was stopped before the women could finish their last test. Was this because of sexism? Maybe the men became afraid that the women were equal, or sometimes better, than them.

An astronaut training in water

Today, Wally Funk has thousands of flight hours, and she has taught over 3,000 students how to fly. After the Women in Space programme, women started to go into space, but the first woman was Russian, not American.

Valentina Tereshkova was the first woman astronaut to go into space. She was chosen from 400 people to pilot *Vostok 6* on 16th June 1963. She is still the only woman who has been on a journey into space alone. She was twenty-six.

Valentina Tereshkova (1937–present)

Valentina was born in a village about 170 miles from Moscow. Her parents worked on a farm, and her father was killed during World War Two. Valentina left school when she was sixteen and worked at a factory, but she continued her education in the evenings. She also learned how to jump from an aeroplane with a parachute. She loved it.

After Russian Yuri Gagarin became the first man in space in 1961, Valentina became excited. She joined the Russian space programme. She was not a pilot, but she joined the programme because of her 126 parachute jumps. At the time, astronauts had to parachute down when they came back near to Earth. Valentina and four other women had eighteen months of lessons. She did many tests. Of the five women, only Valentina went into space.

The Americans did not send a woman into space until Sally Ride became the first American woman in space in 1983.

Today, it is much easier for women to become astronauts.

An astronaut in a parachute near to Earth

CHAPTER NINE

Women and sport

The modern history of women in sport started in the 19th century. At that time, **golf** and tennis were two of the sports that women played. At the first modern Olympic Games in Athens, Greece, in 1896, there were no women. Women first went to the Olympics in Paris, France, in 1900. But only twenty-two women played in those Games, out of the 997 people from nineteen countries. Women were in only five sports: sailing, golf, equestrian, tennis and croquet.

Little by little, more women's sports were in the Olympics. Women's athletics came in 1928. In 1948, the Olympics came to London, United Kingdom. In these Games, there were more sports that women could take part in. Men decided who could be in which sports.

Statue of Fanny Blankers-Koen (1918–2004) in Rotterdam, Netherlands

One famous woman who was at the London Olympics in 1948 was Fanny Blankers-Koen, an athlete from the Netherlands. She was thirty years old and had two children. People called her "the flying housewife", which is a word for a woman who stays at home to look after her husband and children. Fanny was the top female athlete at the London Olympic Games because she got the most medals.

Fanny was born in 1918 in a small town in the Netherlands. Her father worked for the government, but he was also an athlete. She had five brothers. When she was young, she liked many sports, and she was very good at them. She couldn't decide which sport to choose. Her teacher told her to become a runner. As a runner, she could do great things.

Fanny won a lot of races when she was young. But in 1948 she was thirty years old, and many people thought that she was too old to be the best. Other people said she had to look after her husband and her children! But Fanny started the 1948 Games by winning two races – one of them was the 100 metres. Then she won the 200 metres race and the 4 x 100 metres relay race. When she went home to the Netherlands, the Dutch were very happy. She showed everyone that a woman could

Fanny Blankers-Koen, London Olympics, 1948

be a housewife and still win gold medals! In 1999, Fanny Blankers-Koen was voted Female Athlete of the Century because of her four gold medals at the 1948 Games.

Fanny Blankers-Koen was one of the first women to show that women could also be great athletes. Later, there were other great sportswomen, like American tennis player Billie Jean King.

When Billie Jean King was twelve years old, she decided that she wanted to fight for equal rights for girls and women. And she used tennis to do that.

Billie Jean King was born in 1943 in Long Beach, California, USA. Her family were athletes, and Billie Jean liked sport, too. She asked her father what sport she could play. Her father talked about tennis.

A few months later, Billie Jean's friend took her to play tennis for the first time. As soon as she hit the ball, Billie Jean knew that she wanted to be a tennis player. She began to play at Long Beach, and she used a racquet she bought with money she got from little jobs. Her family were not rich. Still, she told her mother that she was going to be number one in the world. But she soon knew that tennis was different for women than for men.

Billie Jean King (1943–present)

When she was twelve years old, she played at a **tournament** at the Los Angeles Tennis Club, but Billie Jean could not be in the group picture of young tennis players. That was because she wore the short trousers her mother made her wear. She did not wear the usual tennis dress worn by female athletes. This taught her that being a tennis player was more difficult for girls.

When she got older, Billie Jean began winning big tennis tournaments, and in 1966 she achieved her dream. She was number one in the world in women's tennis. She was number one for five years in total (1967–1968, 1971–1972 and 1974).

But Billie Jean saw that women tennis players did not win as much money as men. When she won the US Open tournament in 1972, she received $15,000 less than the men's top player, Ilie Năstase. She would not go to the US Open in 1973 because of that, she said. The US Open became the first big tournament to give equal money to its men and women top players. Wimbledon, the oldest tennis tournament in the sport's history, was the last big tournament to do this, in 2007. Today, tennis is one of the few sports that pays its men and women the same in big tournaments. This is thanks to Billie Jean and other female players like Martina Navratilova and Venus Williams.

In 1973, Billie had another fight. This time it was against a man – his name was Bobby Riggs.

Bobby Riggs was a top men's tennis player in the

1930s and 1940s. He won the Wimbledon men's tournament in 1939, and he was the world number one tennis player in 1941, 1946 and 1947. The women's game was much worse than the men's game, he said. Even he – a fifty-five-year-old man – could win against the best female players. He played the Australian player Margaret Court. Bobby Riggs won easily. Then, Billie Jean agreed to play him.

The Riggs–King **match** happened in Texas on 20th September 1973. There were 30,492 people at the match. Also, about 50 million people watched it on TV in the USA, and about 90 million in thirty-seven other countries watched it. The twenty-nine-year-old Billie Jean beat the fifty-five-year-old Bobby 6–4, 6–3, 6–3. She won $100,000. Billie Jean knew that the match was very important for women's rights.

Billie Jean King and Bobby Riggs, 1973

In her tennis career, Billie Jean won thirty-nine big tournament titles. She was one of the greatest tennis players ever. But she did not just play tennis; she also made great progress for women's equality and for women's pay in sport. On 28th August 2006, the United States Tennis Association (USTA) National Tennis Center was named the USTA Billie Jean King National Tennis Center.

In many countries, women's fight to be in sports has taken longer. In Saudi Arabia, for example, it was 2012 when two women went to the Olympics for the first time. Their names were Sarah Attar and Wojdan Shaherkani. Sarah ran the 800 metres, and Wojdan was in the judo.

Sarah Attar (1992–present), London Olympics, 2012

Since 1980, in Iran, the government has not allowed women into stadiums to see all-men sports. But now, things are changing. In June 2018, the Azadi Stadium's doors were opened to women and men during the last two Iran games at the 2018 World Cup.

Things are changing fast in the world. Women have fought for the right to watch sports, to practise them and to enter tournaments.

CHAPTER TEN

Women and empowerment

In 2016, the United Nations (UN) introduced some goals for our future and for the future of the Earth. The goals are there to stop people from being poor, to look after the Earth and to stop war. They are called the Sustainable Development Goals.

Goal Five is about equality between all genders. This goal talks about **empowering** women, which means helping them to become stronger and braver. All the women in this book have felt **empowered** to achieve great things, and they have helped to empower other women.

The history of women's **empowerment** is long, and a lot of progress has been made. But there are still many things that stop women from enjoying an equal life.

Sustainable Development Goal Five

In some parts of the world, for example, very young girls have to get married. This is called "child marriage". More than 700 million women in the world today were married before the age of eighteen. 250 million were married before fifteen!

This is often because families are poor. Parents in poor families marry girls when they are young so they do not have to give them food at home. Sometimes, they also get money from the parents of their daughter's husband.

In sub-Saharan Africa, 40% of women are married as children. For example, 32% of girls in Zimbabwe get married before they are eighteen years old. Loveness Mudzuru and Ruvimbo Tsopodzi were two young women from Zimbabwe who were married to men when they were sixteen years old. Loveness had two children before she was eighteen. Ruvimbo's husband hit her, and sometimes she had to sleep outside. She said, "I wanted to stay in school but he **refused**. It was very, very terrible."

Loveness and Ruvimbo decided that they had to do something about child marriage. They took the government of Zimbabwe to court. The law was bad, they said – the lowest age for boys to marry was eighteen, but the lowest age for girls was sixteen.

Girls fighting against child marriage in Mozambique, sub-Saharan Africa

On 20th January 2016, after many months of thinking and talking, the court changed the law. Now, the lowest age to get married in Zimbabwe is eighteen, and it's the same for boys and girls. The two young women were very brave, and they were empowered. They helped to make a big change in their country.

#MeToo signs at a women's march in Philadelphia, USA

Progress is coming slowly to other countries. In Guatemala and Malawi, for example, the lowest age for marriage is now higher. Nepal and Zambia are working on laws that help girls. But the big problem in any country is changing the way people think about child marriage – and that takes time.

One of the biggest stories of women's empowerment has come with the #MeToo movement, which started in 2017. #MeToo is a movement against sexual harassment and assault.

#MeToo was used a lot from October 2017 on social media to show that there is a lot of sexual assault and harassment of women, everywhere in the world. At the same time, famous men in the film business, like Harvey Weinstein, were accused of harassing and assaulting women – and men in TV and politics have also been accused of these crimes. In 2018, a very famous man in American TV, Bill Cosby, was **convicted** of sexual assault and was sent to prison for three to ten years.

The words "Me Too" were first used by an American woman called Tarana Burke in 2006. They were used again by actor Alyssa Milano in 2017. Alyssa told women to write about sexism and harassment on social media to show how big the problem was. That night, social media became very busy, as #MeToo started everywhere in the world.

At the end of that day, there were movements in many languages, like Arabic, Farsi, French, Hindi and Spanish.

Today, women in many different countries are using #MeToo every day to tell people about the assault and harassment they get. They are asking for change.

Many famous women said "Me Too" – Hollywood actors like Gwyneth Paltrow, Ashley Judd, Jennifer Lawrence and Uma Thurman have all said it. Because of this, everyone learned that there is a lot of sexual assault in the film business. More than 300 women from Hollywood got together and started a group called "Time's Up". They asked for money for women who have been sexually assaulted. 17,700,000 women say that they have been sexually harassed or assaulted since 1998.

Time magazine gave the "Person of the Year" for 2017 to the brave women who spoke about the problem of sexual harassment and assault.

In many countries, it is very difficult for women to talk about sexual assault. Many women became brave because they saw other brave women in the #MeToo movement. They chose to speak after other women spoke out.

In Japan, for example, the #MeToo movement started small, but it is getting bigger. Buzzfeed Japan, which is a news website, has started a #MeToo page with stories about the movement in Japan. Today, the #MeToo movement is very big everywhere. Women have started really talking about sexual harassment, which is a big problem in their lives.

In the 21st century, women are stronger and braver than ever. They still need to make progress. But thanks to the women in this book – and others – women are now much more equal in society than they have ever been before.

During-reading questions

Write the answers to these questions in your notebook.

CHAPTER ONE

1 When was Mary Wollstonecraft born? 1759

2 What prize did Malala Yousafzai win? Nobel Peace Prize

CHAPTER TWO

1 Why is Rosa Parks famous? Didn't stand up in the bus

2 What was Shirin Ebadi's job in 1975? Why was this special? First President of City Court

3 Which country does Rigoberta Menchú come from?

Guatemala

CHAPTER THREE

1 What was the name of the leader of the suffragettes?

2 How did Emily Davison die?

CHAPTER FOUR

1 When did the third and fourth waves of feminism start?

2 Simone de Beauvoir wrote about the difference between sex and gender. What is it?

3 What is the #MeToo movement?

CHAPTER FIVE

1 Do you agree with these sentences? Why/Why not?

a During World Wars One and Two, more women went to work outside the home.

b Women's work has not changed since World War Two.

c Women earn as much money as men.

CHAPTER SIX

1 Why is Marie Curie famous?

2 Which woman scientist helped to discover how DNA is made?

3 What did Tu Youyou discover?

CHAPTER SEVEN

1 What job did Nancy Astor do?
2 Which country did the first woman prime minister come from?
3 Why is Jacinda Ardern famous?

CHAPTER EIGHT

1 What was Amelia Earhart doing when she disappeared?
2 Who was the first woman astronaut in space?
3 What year did the first American woman go into space?

CHAPTER NINE

1 How did Billie Jean King make progress for women in sport?
2 When did Saudi Arabian women go to the Olympics for the first time?

CHAPTER TEN

1 Do you agree with these sentences? Why/Why not?
   a Many girls in the world get married too young.
   b Women in the film business started the "Time's Up" group.
   c The #MeToo movement is only important in the USA.

After-reading questions

1 Which woman's story did you like the most? Why?
2 Do you think it's important for girls and young women to know about these women who have changed the world? Why/Why not?
3 Look back at your answer to "Before-reading question 2". Do you feel the same way after reading the book?

Exercises

CHAPTER ONE

1 Are these sentences *true* or *false*? Write the correct answers in your notebook.

1. Women have always been educated. ....*false*............
2. Catherine the Great started free education for girls in Russia.
3. Mary Wollstonecraft is known as "the mother of British feminism".
4. Malala Yousafzai wrote for an American news website.
5. Malala was shot by the government.
6. Millions of girls around the world do not go to school.

CHAPTER TWO

2 Write the correct answers in your notebook.

Example: *1 – b*

1 Harriet Tubman ran away from the south of the USA . . .
  a to be with her family.
  b to find freedom.
  c because she killed someone.

2 Who did not stand up on a bus in 1955?
  a Rigoberta Menchú
  b Shirin Ebadi
  c Rosa Parks

3 Shirin Ebadi studied . . .
  a mathematics.
  b law.
  c English.

4 Rigoberta Menchú fought for . . .
  a the rights of all Guatemalan people.
  b the rights of soldiers.
  c the rights of Indigenous people in Guatemala.

CHAPTER THREE

3 Complete these sentences in your notebook, using the words from the box.

government	vote	allowed	brave
forced	arrested	leader	

1 Emmeline Pankhurst was the ....*leader*........... of the fight for women to vote in Britain.
2 In 1913, the .... would not give women the vote.
3 Emily Davison was very .... when she threw herself in front of a horse.
4 Emmeline Pankhurst was .... fifteen times.
5 The police sometimes .... the suffragettes to eat.
6 Italian women got the .... in 1945.
7 In 2018, Saudi Arabian women were .... to drive.

CHAPTERS FOUR AND FIVE

4 Write the correct words in your notebook.

1	armstnehas	Sexual .....*harassment*..... is a crime.
2	oeohppihslr	Simone de Beauvoir's job
3	edregn	This is made by society, says Simone de Beauvoir.
4	imfneism	a movement that wants to achieve equality between all people
5	Islma	a religion
6	lpito	a person who flies a plane
7	zaiegnma	something that you read
8	coslai diaem	Facebook, Twitter, Instagram, etc.

CHAPTER SIX

5 Complete these sentences in your notebook, using the words from the box.

for	from	in	of	with

1 In the past, women worked ....*in*.............. other people's homes.
2 Marie Curie is one of the big names .... the 20th century.
3 Marie Curie came .... Poland.
4 Lisa Meitner worked .... Otto Hahn.
5 Tu Youyou discovered a medicine .... malaria.

CHAPTER SEVEN

6 Match the two parts of these sentences in your notebook.

1 Nancy Astor was an
2 In 1928, British women
3 The first female prime minister
4 Hillary Clinton wanted to
5 In 2017, Rwanda had the most female
6 Jacinda Ardern was the
7 Benazir Bhutto was the first woman
8 People hope that, in the future, 50% of the world's

a to have a baby while in office.
b MPs in the world.
c world's youngest female prime minister.
d become president in 2016.
e got the vote at twenty-one.
f governments will be women.
g MP until 1945.
h came from Sri Lanka.

CHAPTER EIGHT

7 Order the words to make sentences in your notebook.

1 lots / different / of / jobs / Amelia / had
Amelia had lots of different jobs.
2 In / spoke / morning / Earhart / radio / the / on / the
3 pilots / USA / had / women / many / The
4 woman / The / was / first / Russian / astronaut
5 went / alone / space / Tereshkova / into
6 now / easier / women / It / for / much / go / to / space / into / is

CHAPTER TEN

8 Read the answers, and write the correct question words in your notebook.

1 ......*What*...... are the Sustainable Development Goals?
The Sustainable Development Goals stop people from being poor, look after the Earth and stop war from happening.
2 .... did the UN introduce the goals?
In 2016.
3 .... took the government of Zimbabwe to court?
Loveness Mudzuru and Ruvimbo Tsopodzi.
4 .... countries are working on laws that help girls?
Nepal and Zambia.
5 .... was convicted of sexual assault?
Bill Cosby.
6 .... Hollywood actors supported the #MeToo movement?
Gwyneth Paltrow, Ashley Judd, Jennifer Lawrence and Uma Thurman.

Project work

1 Choose one of the women in this book. Look online to find out more about her. Make a poster, and include information about her life, what she has achieved and why she is important.

2 In this book, you read about women who changed the world. Find out more about women in your country. Write a news story about a "women's problem" in your country, or about a famous woman who has changed your society. Show your work to your friends.

3 Do you agree or disagree with these sentences? Write your answers.

a Women in my country earn as much as men.
b Women in my country control their own money.
c Women in my country can have good jobs. They can be pilots, astronauts, lawyers, etc.
d Things are better for women in my country now than in the past.

4 What are the three most important difficulties that women still have? How can they be solved? Make a short presentation to give to your friends.

5 Make a short TV news item about one of the events in this book.

An answer key for all questions and exercises can be found at **www.penguinreaders.co.uk**

Glossary

accuse (v)
to say that a person has done something wrong

arrest (v)
If someone is *arrested*, the police stop them and take them away.

career (n)
the most important job or jobs that you do through your life

century (n)
a hundred years

chemistry (n); **chemist** (n)
an area of *science*. *Chemistry* helps us understand how to make medicines, for example.

convict (v)
to send someone to prison

court (n)
a place where people decide if a person will go to prison

democracy (n)
In a country that has *democracy*, the people choose the government.

divorce (n and v)
when people who are married decide not to be together any more

earn (v)
to get money from a job

education (n); **educate** (v)
when you learn about things

election (n); **elect** (v)
There is an *election* in a country when people choose their government.

empower (v);
empowered (adj);
empowerment (n)
to help someone to be strong and brave. This is *empowerment*.

equality (n); **equal** (adj)
when all people get the same thing or the same amount of a thing

female (adj)
a sex. A person, animal or plant can be *female*.

feminist (adj and n)
someone who believes that all genders are equally important and should have the same things

flight (n)
travelling in and flying planes

force (v)
to make someone do something even if they say no

free (adj); **freely** (adv);
freedom (n)
People are *free* when they can do what they want; people can speak *freely* when they can say what they want. This is *freedom*. Something is also *free* if you do not have to pay money for it.

gender (n)
Your *gender* is if you are a man, a woman, both or neither.

goal (n)
Your *goal* is the thing that you want to do or be.

golf (n)
a sport where you hit a small white ball into holes in the ground

government (n)
a group of important people who decide what must happen in a country

harassment (n); **harass** (v)
When someone often does or says things to you that you do not like, they *harass* you. This is *harassment.*

health (n)
The way your body feels. If you feel well, you are in good *health.* If you feel ill, you are in bad *health.*

history (n); **historian** (n)
History is all the things that happened before now. A person who knows a lot about *history* is an *historian.*

Indigenous (adj)
An *Indigenous* person comes from the place where they are living.

Islam (n)
Islamic people believe in *Islam.* They learn and follow the things that Muhammad said.

law (n); **lawyer** (n)
The *law* is what is right and wrong in a country. A *lawyer* helps people with the *law.*

lead (v); **leader** (n)
If you *lead* a group of people, they follow you, and they do what you tell them. You are their *leader.*

malaria (n)
You can get *malaria* from a small insect in some hot countries. If you have *malaria*, you are very ill.

marriage (n)
when two people promise to love each other and stay together for all of their lives

match (n)
a game of tennis or football, for example

Member of Parliament (MP) (pr n)
a person who works in the *government*

movement (n)
a group of people who work together to change something important in the world

perilous (adj)
dangerous

philosopher (n); **philosophy** (n)
A *philosopher* studies life and what it means. This is *philosophy.*

physics (n)
an area of science. *Physics* helps us to understand how things move, for example.

politics (n); **politician** (n)
A *politician* is a person who works in the *government.* A *politician* works in the world of *politics.*

president (n)
the *leader* of a country without a king or queen

prime minister (n)
the most important *Member of Parliament* in a country

professor (n)
an important teacher at a university

programme (n)
a plan that people follow to learn or achieve something

progress (n)
When you make *progress*, you start to get what you want.

publisher (n); **publish** (v)
If someone *publishes* books, they make and sell books. A *publisher* makes and sells books.

race (n)
a group of people who may share some of the same things, like their *history* or parts of what they look like

radioactivity (n)
something that is used to make X-rays (= photographs that help a doctor to see inside your body)

refuse (v)
to say no to doing something

rights (n)
the things that everyone must be allowed to have or do

rule (v)
to *lead* other people and tell them what to do

science (n)
When you study *science*, you learn about the way the world works.

sexism (n)
When someone thinks that you are not important because of your gender, this is *sexism*.

sexual assault (n)
when someone touches or attacks the private parts of another person's body

sexuality (n)
A person's *sexuality* tells you which gender, or genders, they prefer to have sex with.

social (adj); **society** (n)
Society is people living together in a country. *Social* problems sometimes happen between these people.

test (v and n)
If you take a *test*, you have to answer questions or do something to show that you are good enough. If someone *tests* you, you do this, and then they decide if you are good enough.

tournament (n)
In a *tournament*, people play a lot of *matches*. The winners play against other winners. In the end, there is only one team left. This team is the winner of the *tournament*.

unique (adj)
the only one of something

wave (n)
A *wave* is a line of high water that moves in the sea. We talk about a *wave* when there is a big change in the way people think or do things.

#MeToo (n)
a phrase used on social media. The word for # is "hashtag".

Photo credits

Cover and page 51 (Amelia Earhart) ©New York Times Co./Getty Images; cover and page 15 (Harriet Tubman) Library of Congress, Prints & Photographs Division/Harvey B Lindsley/LC-USZ62-7816 DLC; cover and page 31 (Betty Friedan) Library of Congress, Prints & Photographs Division/ World Telegram & Sun photo by Fred Palumbo/ LC-USZ62-115884; cover (Hillary Clinton) ©Sipa/Shutterstock; cover and page 38 (Carrie Gracie) Courtesy of Wikimedia/Joi Ito/CC BY 2.0 https://creativecommons.org/licenses/by/2.0/deed.en; cover and page 11 (Malala Yousafzai) copyright ©Simon Davis/ DFID/CC BY 3.0/Open Government License/http://www.nationalarchives.gov.uk/doc/open-government-licence/ version/3/; cover and page 32 (Nawal El Saadawi) Courtesy of Wikimedia/Boberger Foto Bengt Oberger /CC BY 3.0/ https://creativecommons.org/licenses/by/3.0/deed.en; cover and pages 4 and 17 (judge Shirin Ebadi) Courtesy of Wikimedia/Vogler/ CC BY-SA 4.0 https://creativecommons.org/licenses/by-sa/4.0/deed.en; cover and page 37 (Sheryl Sandberg) © Krista Kennell/Shutterstock.com; cover and page 15 (Rosa Parks) copyright ©Photo12/UIG/Getty Images; cover and page 30 (Simone de Beauvoir) copyright ©Sipa/REX/Shutterstock; cover and page 20 (Emmeline Pankhurst) Emmeline Pankhurst by Chicago Matzene/National Woman's Party Records, Group II, Container II:275, Folder: Individual Photographs Nos. 301-349 "P",http://hdl.loc.gov/loc.mss/mnwp.275016/ Library of Congress, Washington, D.C; cover and page 47 (Sirimavo Bandaranaike) copyright ©Murali/Pix Inc./The LIFE Images Collection/Getty Images; cover and pages 4 and 58 (Fanny Blankers-Koen) ©Mark Kauffman/The LIFE Picture Collection/Getty Images; cover and page 46 (Nancy Astor) copyright © ullstein bild Dtl./Getty Images; cover and page 34 (women working at a house) copyright ©S W A Newton/ English Heritage/Arcaid/Corbis via Getty Images; cover and page 44 (Emily Levesque) copyright © Emily Levesque/ Photographer: David Pitman; cover and page 35 (women making guns) Courtesy of Wikimedia/DAVID HOLT/ CC BY-SA 2.0/https://creativecommons.org/licenses/by-sa/2.0/deed.en; cover and page 9 (Mary Wollstonecraft) copyright © Art Collection 2 / Alamy Stock Photo; cover and page 54 (Wally Funk) copyright ©99s Museum of Women Pilots, Oklahoma City, OK; cover and page 8 (Catharine Macaulay) copyright ©The Picture Art Collection / Alamy Stock Photo; cover and page 8 (Catherine the Great) copyright ©Universal History Archive/Getty Images; cover and page 27 (Hatoon al-Fassi) copyright ©REUTERS/Fahad Shadeed (SAUDI ARABIA); pages 4 and 55 (astronaut) copyright ©Sovfoto/UIG via Getty Images; page 4 (judo) Courtesy of Wikimedia/Martin Hesketh/CC BY 2.0/https://creativecommons.org/licenses/by/2.0/deed.en; page 4 (magazine) © lentamart/Shutterstock.com; page 4 (medicine) © Bukhta Yurii/Shutterstock.com; pages 5 and 36 (pilot Nillofar Rahmani) Courtesy of Staff Sgt. Scott Saldukas/United States Air Force/130513-F-ZE564-077; page 5 (stadium) Courtesy of Wikimedia/Vathlu/CC BY-SA 4.0/https://creativecommons.org/licenses/by-sa/4.0/deed/en; pages 5 and 57 (statue of Fanny Blankers-Koen) Courtesy of Wikimedia/Ruud Zwart/CC BY-SA 2.5 NL/https://creativecommons.org/licenses/by-sa/2.5/nl/deed.en; page 5 (university) © istock.com/travelview; pages 5 and 26 (vote) copyright ©Ahmed Yosri/EPA/REX/ Shutterstock; page 10 (A Vindication of the Rights of Woman) Library of Congress Rare Books & Special Collections Division, Washington/LC-USZ62-61444; page 10 (Mary Wollstonecraft's picture on Houses of Parliament) Courtesy of Wikimedia/ NeilWissink/CC BY-SA 3.0/https://creativecommons.org/licenses/by-sa/3.0/deed.en; pages 12–13 (Malala with President Obama) copyright ©Pete Souza/The White House via Getty Images; page 18 (Rigoberta Menchú) Courtesy of Flickr/Carlos Rodriguez/Archivo Medios Públicos EP/ CC BY-SA 2.0/https://creativecommons.org/licenses/by-sa/2.0/; page 21 (Emmeline Pankhurst speaking in New York) copyright ©Granger Historical Picture Archive / Alamy Stock Photo; page 22 (woman being forced to eat) copyright ©Bettmann/Getty Images; page 29 (Huda Shaarawi) Courtesy of Wikimedia Commons; page 33 (Laura Bates) copyright ©David Levenson/Getty Images; page 35 (Rosie the Riveter) © TinaImages/shutterstock. com; page 39 (Marie Curie) Library of Congress, Prints & Photographs Division,/LC-B2- 1397-7; page 40 (Curie with Einstein) Courtesy of Wikimedia Commons/Institut International de Physique Solvay; page 42 (X-ray) Courtesy of Wikimedia/Aidan Jones/ CC BY-SA 2.0 https://creativecommons.org/licenses/by-sa/2.0/deed.en; page 42 (Lise Meitner) Courtesy of Smithsonian Institution/Flickr/Acc. 90-105 - Science Service, Records, 1920s-1970s, Smithsonian Institution Archives; page 43 (Rosalind Franklin) copyright ©Science History Images / Alamy Stock Photo; page 43 (DNA) © Iaremenko Sergii/shutterstock.com; page 44 (Tu Youyou) copyright ©Historic Collection / Alamy Stock Photo; page 45 (Houses of Parliament) Courtesy of Flickr/Shane Global/CC BY 2.0/https://creativecommons.org/licenses/by/2.0/; page 48 (Hillary Clinton) Courtesy of U.S. State Department; page 50 (Jacinda Ardern) Courtesy of Wikimedia/Government House, New Zealand/ CC By 4.0/https://creativecommons.org/licenses/by/4.0/deed.en; page 54 (astronaut in water) copyright ©Bill Brassard (NBL)/NASA; page 56 (astronaut and parachute) copyright ©NASA/Getty Images; page 58 (Fanny Blankers-Koen) copyright ©Mark Kauffman/The LIFE Picture Collection/Getty Images; page 59 (Billie Jean King) copyright ©Associated Newspapers /REX/Shutterstock; page 61 (Billie Jean King and Bobby Riggs) copyright ©Everett Collection Inc / Alamy Stock Photo; page 62 (Sarah Attar) copyright ©John G Mabanglo/EPA/REX/Shutterstock; page 64 (Sustainable Development Goal Five) Courtesy of UNDP Europe http://www.undp.org/content/undp/en/home/sustainable-development-goals.html; page 65 (girls fighting against child marriage) Courtesy of Plan International; page 66 (#MeToo signs) Courtesy of Wikimedia/ Rob Kall/CC BY 2.0/https://creativecommons.org/licenses/by/2.0/deed.en